MADE FOR

More

LIFE BEYOND THE WRECKAGE OF HURT, LOSS, AND HEARTBREAK

A Bible Study Experience for Single Moms
(& Anyone Else Whose Life Hasn't Gone as Planned)

Michelle Donnelly
with Callie Beukinga

TESTIMONY

MEDIA GROUP

Made for More: Life Beyond the Wreckage of Hurt, Loss, and Heartbreak

A Bible Study Experience for Single Moms
(& Anyone Else Whose Life Hasn't Gone as Planned)

Copyright © 2023 by Michelle Donnelly

Published by Testimony Media Group
Published with the assistance of The Wayne Hastings Co., LLC
Cover and interior design by Jorie Lee

Contents

The journey

is long,

but my friend,

you are going

to make it.

Introduction

I can't stand when people talk in the middle of a movie. Ugh, it makes me crazy—one of my all-time pet peeves. My first-born does this often, and sometimes I think she does it just because she knows it really gets my goat.

(Okay, I have to admit—I've been known to do the same kind of thing myself. That apple did not fall far from this tree.)

Aside from her fondness for aging me prematurely, my firstborn is also super into history. When she turned thirteen, she became enthralled with the story of the RMS Titanic. When I was about her age I also went through a "Titanic" phase, but if you're anywhere around middle age you already know this obsession had something to do with the release of the Kate and Leo epic, *Titanic*. How Hollywood managed to turn an international tragedy into one of the most popular love stories of all time, I'll never know. It's kind of weird if you think about it, but we all *totally* bought it.

And I do mean *bought* it. I loved the movie so much I went to the theatre *three times* to watch the three-hour long film. I ordered a cheap knock-off of Rose's necklace from a teen magazine (which I never wore because I was far too embarrassed to admit I actually had it). And because these were the days before streaming, I spent $12.99 on the entire CD soundtrack just so I could listen to "My Heart Will Go On," on repeat. I wanted to relive the experience again and again—not of watching a tragic love story but of being transported to another time and place.

For that reason, I knew my daughter would appreciate the film too, and I figured with a little strategic fast-forwarding we could enjoy a mother/daughter movie night together. I recovered our dusty old DVD player from a box in the garage along with my original DVD copy of *Titanic*. We settled on the couch with our popcorn and a couple of Cokes, but it wasn't long after I pressed play that my daughter started in with the questions.

"I thought this was a movie about Rose sailing on the Titanic. Why is she an old lady?"

I chuckled and explained to her, "Just keep watching."

"Why is she with that guy? The DVD cover shows her with that other guy."

I smiled and explained to her, "Just keep watching."

"So she obviously lives if she's an old lady in the story. Does Jack make it to New York with her?"

Of course you know what I said: "Just keep watching."

Sometimes, we live life like this. When we're hit by hurt and heartbreak, we want to try to make sense of things as quickly as possible. We want to bypass the unfolding of the story and just skip to the end. I think we think if we can just explain things away, somehow the aching of our souls will stop and everything will be like it was, or like we wanted it to be.

But we know life doesn't work like that. There are some things we just can't explain, and when we try we become angrier or more disappointed than we were at the start. We hit a crossroads where the tug of the future, of a story that is still being written forces us to loosen our grip on an unexplainable past. It's the only way we can make room for the possibilities of the unknown.

We can't always understand the story when we're in the middle of it. It's in that moment we have to consider: "Is there more out there for me? Could there be more ahead than what lies behind?"

Even if you decide the answer is yes, moving ahead doesn't mean you won't have fear about how the story is going to unfold. In fact, you're very likely to have fear if the story you thought you were living is suddenly interrupted, or if things up to this point haven't gone so well in the first place. But God can work with that. You don't need to have it all figured out to take the next step. And sometimes, the next step is simply being willing to "just keep watching."

I know, easier said than done. But the courage we need to step forward in our stories doesn't come from within ourselves. It is given to us by the One who holds the pen.

I'll admit, being willing to wait on what God is doing is pretty scary when we don't really know who God is or if we can trust Him. We may ask, "Where was He then? Hasn't He been holding the pen the whole time? What happened?"

And you know what? God can handle all of your questions. He invites our confusion because He wants to make things clear. But that means when it comes to our own stories, we often have to keep walking, keep watching, and keep waiting to see what God is revealing in real time.

The reason this is so challenging for us is that unlike a movie, our stories don't exactly unfold in a straight line. Though we may start moving forward, at some point we all have to go backward in our stories before we can continue on. There are things we have to deal with from the past that are tripping us up and blocking the way to what God has for us in the future. But other times, when the past is too overwhelming to revisit, God will invite us to take a few steps forward to discover the safety and security we need to eventually go backward. Whichever seems truest for you in this moment, know that both are part of the healing journey.

I know sometimes it feels like you're wandering and not making much progress, but God is leading you at the pace He knows is best for you. This Bible study experience is designed to help you understand Him as your good and gentle Guide, and to teach you how to find rest for your soul along the way. The journey is long, but my friend, you are going to make it.

In the meantime, you may start to wonder who this God is and what He is doing. The good news is God wants you to know who He is and what He is doing! It brings Him joy to lead His children to the answers and one of the best places to find them is in the Bible. When we read the Bible, we see the stories of other desperate, despairing, and disappointed people just like us. Their stories are just like ours, but because these people have gone before us we get to see how things turned out for them in the end. We can see through each life how God reveals exactly who He is, and how He delights in *proving* Himself again and again as our stories also unfold.

We have to know this: the stories we read in the Bible are *not* the tales of people who simply "got lucky." They are the experiences of completely ordinary people, like you and me, that show us who God really is and what He's up to in our pain and disappointment. Through them, we can borrow their faith, knowing the God who came through for them is coming through for us too. He is the same God, and these stories are not the exception. They are the rule.

I'm proud of you for deciding to take this journey. It takes courage to take God at His Word. It takes daring to believe that the story that's already been written isn't the whole picture, that there could be more ahead . . . that there could be *goodness* ahead. But even if you feel your courage and daring has long run dry, not to worry. You can definitely get by on a whole lot of curiosity.

Just keep watching.

With you in prayer,
Michelle

Invite

God

to meet

with

you.

How to Use this Book

You may have noticed that I referenced this book as a "Bible study experience." Hebrews 4:12 says the Word of God is "alive and active," which means it's so much more than a collection of stories. The Bible is God's power on a page, and when it gets inside of us it works on and in us to change our lives.

Because it's alive, we can interact with it and experience it. We can feel its power working on the broken parts of our lives. But I'll admit; that isn't exactly the easiest or most straightforward thing. Most of us aren't taught how to connect with the Bible, and sometimes our past experiences have made Bible reading seem like an intimidating, threatening, or frustrating thing. Maybe you have the impression that the average person just can't read the Bible for themselves. Maybe the Bible seems like a big old book of rules with a lot of unfamiliar names in it, written so long ago that it's hard to understand what's going on. Or maybe it's been used to harm and shame you, and you're afraid of what more condemnation and criticism you'll find.

Whatever your story, we want to help you clear away the roadblocks and simplify the process of getting to know God and yourself better through His Word.

You'll notice that each of the six chapters of this book has the same five parts:

 Story summary

 Memory verse/ word study

 Reflection Questions

 Practice

 Family Focus

We recommend choosing a 30-day or six-week plan for this Bible study experience. If you're using the 30-day method, you'll read one section of one chapter each day. If you're choosing the six-week model (a great idea for a small group study), you can cover one chapter each week.

This is your time, so savor it in whatever way you can. Grab a coffee or your favorite cup of tea. Light a candle or wrap yourself up in a favorite blanket. As you settle in each time, invite God to meet with you. Ask Him to show you something new. Distractions and interruptions are to be expected, but know you can always dive right back in whenever you get off track. He's always there waiting, eager to spend time with you.

Teaching videos for this study available at
plusoneparents.org/resources

"For I know the plans I have for you," says the LORD. "They are plans for good and not for disaster,

to give you a future and a hope."

JEREMIAH 29:11 (NLT)

CHAPTER 1

Made for More Than What You've Been Told

 *Eve*

When I was newly divorced, I took up hiking as a hobby. I needed a way to pass the lonely weekends without my kids and to prove to myself that I really could do something alone (not easy for this extrovert).

A seasoned former Girl Scout, I always made sure I arrived at the trailhead prepared. Backpack? Check. Extra socks? Check. Favorite snacks? Check.

After parking, I'd take a look at the trail map to pick my route. Before setting out, I'd always take a picture of the map so I'd have it handy in case I ever got turned around. After completing several successful hikes, I figured I knew the park's trail system well enough and set out one afternoon, boldly deciding I didn't need to take a picture of the trail map anymore.

As I trekked along, I thought it strange how many fewer hikers were on the trails that day. I continued on, although less confident that if I needed help anyone would be around to assist me. I kept on my course until suddenly; I hit an unfamiliar fork in the trail.

This isn't supposed to be here, I thought to myself. I looked round, but didn't see anything I recognized. Though I stood for a few minutes, no one else came by. And in the eerie stillness, I glanced upward through the trees and noticed dusk had begun sneaking up on the afternoon sky.

A wave of hot panic flushed over me—I was lost.

After whimper crying for a few minutes (and getting mad at myself for not taking a picture of the map before I left), I remembered seeing a trail map about a mile back up the way I came. Several wrong turns later, I finally found it. Confidently it declared, "You are here!"

Frustrated, I stomped my foot and yelled out loud at the sign, "But I don't want to be 'here'!"

Life can feel like that sometimes. One day you wake up in circumstances you never thought you'd be in and think, *"Where am I? How did I even get 'here'?"*

However you landed in the season of life you find yourself in right now, I know you're not here because you planned on it. Maybe you've looked at your life and thought, "I never wanted this to be my story. It's not supposed to be this way."

What would you say if I told you that God agrees with you?

To explain what I mean, we have to go all the way back to the beginning of God's story, to the Garden of Eden. There in the Garden, God created mankind to experience only perfect harmony, peace, beauty, wholeness, and well-being. When we look at the original Hebrew language of the Genesis story, the combination of these attributes is wrapped up into a single, beautiful word: *shalom*.[1]

But we know at the Fall that all changed. Adam and Eve ate of the forbidden fruit and were sent out of the Garden. And now here we all are—suffering and struggling in a broken, fallen world.

As a kid, I remember being in Sunday school and thinking, "Well, Adam and Eve ate the fruit and got punished for it. We all got punished for it." End of story.

But it wasn't the end of the story; it was actually the beginning of something new. It's true, Adam and Eve were sent out of the Garden when they disobeyed God. But the reason, God's *intention* for sending Adam and Eve away, is probably very different than what you've been told before. And it's so important that we re-examine their story because it tells us a lot about the heart of God for us as His children in our own broken circumstances.

Let's look back at the scene. If we could place ourselves in the creation story, we'd see that Adam and Eve enjoyed perfect *shalom* with God and each other in the Garden. They rolled through tall grasses and took in breath-taking sunsets, with no fears or worries to spoil the fun.

Meanwhile, the serpent watched from the wings with ferocious jealousy. You see, he had his shot at enjoying eternity with God, but he blew it. Ever since the moment he fell from glory, his one desire has been to ruin *shalom* for all of us. So he slithered onto the scene, deceived Eve, and tricked her into taking a bite of the forbidden fruit. And as we all know, Adam followed suit.

But the way Eve was deceived is important to take note of; the devil gas lit her. Gaslighting is a manipulative tactic meant to cause someone to doubt reality. Said more simply, it's when someone makes you feel crazy for believing something that is actually true. Gaslighting is always done on purpose, with the intention of opening the door to chaos and confusion—the opposite of *shalom*. The victim is then left unstable and unsure of the situation and themselves.

Perhaps you have experienced this before.

When Eve explained to the devil they were not to eat of the tree for fear of losing their lives, he told her, "You will not surely die. For God knows that when you eat of it your eyes will be opened, and you will be like God, knowing good and evil." Satan basically said to her, "Are you sure? I don't think you have your facts right, honey." The devil questioned Eve's reality, and once she was thoroughly confused and unable to make sense of the whole thing, he went in for the kill. He convinced her that there was more out there for her, but that God didn't want her to have it. And you know what? That enemy is still telling all of us the same thing.

Adam and Eve ate from a tree that has an interesting name; it was called the Tree of the Knowledge of Good and Evil. Adam and Eve were told not to eat from the tree because eating of it would give them a knowledge of evil they were never meant to have. In God's original plan, none of us were ever made to know or experience evil.

But once they ate from the tree, the awareness of evil

crept in, darkening their souls. And instead of *shalom* being the legacy they had to pass on to us, sin and death became our inheritance instead.

As if this was not bad enough, there was *another* tree in the Garden. This tree was called the tree of life. The tree of life granted eternal life to anyone who ate from it. Before the Fall, Adam and Eve were permitted to eat from this tree. But once Adam and Eve were in a fallen state, eating of this tree would have meant that they'd remain eternally fallen—forever—and God did not want that for them, or for any of us.

If you've ever had to hide your dark chocolate from your kids, you know the problem with keeping kids away from the things they aren't supposed to eat. Adam and Eve didn't have the greatest track record when it came to resisting forbidden trees, so they couldn't stay in the Garden without it having major consequences for all mankind.

God prepared clothing for Adam and Eve, and *in His love* for them sent them away. Imagine the grief God felt over this. And to make sure Adam and Eve couldn't get back into the Garden and harm themselves, He blocked the way to the tree with an angel wielding a flaming sword.

Yes, Adam and Eve's choices had consequences. But God's discipline is always with our best interest in mind, and that's what God was doing here. Sending them away wasn't as much about punishment as it was about protection.

But God would not leave things this way. God immediately set His redemption plan in motion to destroy death and evil, restore our innocence, and bring back His original design—to bring back *shalom* and the "more" for which we were created.

When Jesus died on the cross and rose to life, all of that was accomplished. Because of what Jesus has done, *shalom* is ours both now and forever more.

Like drops of rain gathering to form a rushing river, God's *shalom* is becoming more and more true in our lives today, and will be completely true when we are at home in Heaven. But we can't forget that the devil knows this, and that snake is still after every single one of us. His days are numbered, but in the meantime he is at work doing whatever he can to steal *shalom* from us, in this life and the next.

God has already won. And throughout our lives, God is working through everything we experience, the good and the bad, to expose the enemy's schemes, rescue us from the kingdom of darkness, repair the damage done to our souls, and deliver us into His Kingdom of Light. And in doing so, God promises we will be repaid for what we've lost, and receive the power we need to stand against the devil and take back our lives.

As we'll see throughout this journey into God's Word, God uses the hard things of our lives to actually give us an even greater awareness of His *shalom*. In those times when we feel like we have less, He is actually bringing us more. It seems backwards, but that's the way God works.

I know all of this doesn't answer every question of "why," and this doesn't fix the frustration of knowing "You Are Here" when you don't want to be (especially when ending up 'here' was not all your fault). There are no easy answers for things like that. What we do know is that the enemy looks for opportunities to bring us low so he can implant his "alternate explanations" (aka "lies") into each of our hearts, creating confusion around our understanding of Whose we are and who we are.

And I don't know about you, but I am *done* hearing Satan's version of the story.

When we can see the devil's scheme—that since the beginning he's been attacking and deceiving us in his campaign to separate us from our good and adoring Father—we can find the courage to hold all of our unanswered questions in one hand, while leaving the other hand open to see what God might still be up to.[2] Living in the tension between the two can be difficult, but things are made a bit easier when we grasp that God knows it is not supposed to be this way and that He is already at work restoring *shalom* and setting all things right—turning them back to His original design.[3]

God knows you were made for more. The Bible may have wrapped, but God's story didn't. It's still being written in our lives today. And just as the Bible is the story of God coming for all of us and making all things new, your story is too.

FOR FURTHER STUDY, READ GENESIS 1–3

Memory VERSE
"For I know the plans I have for you," says the LORD. "They are plans for good and not for disaster, to give you a future and a hope."
Jeremiah 29:11 (NLT)

God had a plan for Adam and Eve, a plan for good and not disaster. When they made a choice that brought all of us a legacy of shame, God's plan was and is to give us back an inheritance of glory.

This verse in the *New Living Translation* says that God's plans are for "good." The *New International Version* says God's plans are "to prosper you." The *English Standard Version* says God's plans are for "welfare," while the *King James Version* says God's plans are for "peace."

Why are there so many different translations of the same verse? The Hebrew word these translations are drawing from is *shalom*. *Shalom* can be translated so many ways because *shalom* is all of these things: it's goodness, prosperity, welfare, peace, harmony, wholeness, and abundance. It's the state of total perfection for which God designed us and He is breaking into your story to restore it to you, both in this life and in eternity.

Both. And. That's *shalom*, and that's God's plan for you.

 Reflection QUESTIONS

1. How have the things you've experienced in this life caused you to believe that God is punishing you, or that He doesn't want good things for you?

2. How do this week's selection and memory verse
   challenge those thoughts and feelings?

3. Can you think of a time in your past where you saw
   God move? Perhaps even in the way something bad or
   unexpected resulted in something good?

4. How does it make you feel to understand that God knows
   things are not as they should be?

Practice:
EXPERIENCING *SHALOM* IN GOD'S PRESENCE

Sometimes, prayer can feel like we're talking to a faraway God. However, one of the beautiful gifts of being alive on this side of Jesus' resurrection is having access to the Spirit of God with us and *in* us, every minute of every day.

Ephesians 1:13 says, "And when you believed in Christ, He identified you as his own by giving you the Holy Spirit, whom He promised long ago."

Jesus is Immanuel—God with us. While Jesus walked the earth, God's power and presence dwelled *among* His people. But through the Holy Spirit, God's presence and power now dwell *within* His people. And if you are a believer in Christ, this power and presence is already within you, right now. That means you aren't talking to a faraway God, but one who is closer than your next breath.

Learning to connect with God's presence takes practice, but there's incredible peace and power available when we learn to access that presence. Both the Old Testament Hebrew and New Testament Greek words for the Holy Spirit (*ruach* and *pneuma*) actually mean "breath." That means the Spirit of God can be understood as the Breath of God.

What's more, the book of Genesis says God created man from the dust by breathing into him the "breath of life" (Genesis 2:7). God's very breath animates our body and our spirit, and we can become aware of His presence with us by paying attention to His breath inside us.

Stop what you are doing right now and pay attention to the

breath of life within you. Breathe deeply and slowly, acknowledging God's presence within each life-giving breath. Call to mind that it is the Spirit of life and peace that is within you and around you, surrounding you with comfort and strength.

WORSHIP PLAYLIST RECOMMENDATION
"Breathe" by Maverick City Music (featuring Chandler Moore, Jonathan Mc Reynolds, DOE & Mav City Gospel Choir)

 *Family* FOCUS

START THE CONVERSATION

» Ask your child what has been hard for them this week. What do they often feel sad or angry about?

» Let them know that though these emotions are hard, it is normal to feel as they do. If he/she chooses not to share their struggle, let them know that's okay, and that you are always here to talk.

» Share with your child how you have also dealt with sadness or brokenness this week or sometime in the past.

» Explain that God knows we live in a broken world but that He has an amazing rescue plan for us in Jesus. Jesus died on the cross to make a way back to Heaven for us and to repair the brokenness of the world. He came back to life and is alive in Heaven right now. When we believe in Jesus, one day we will join Him in Heaven where there will be no more sadness or hurt. Everything will be perfect, as God originally planned it.

» Ask your child to imagine what a life without sadness and hurt will be like:

> What do you think it will be like if no one said anything mean to you ever again?

> What would it be like if there was no more pain, sickness, or death?

> What do you think Heaven will be like?

ACTIVITY

Grab a Lego set, threads and beads for a friendship bracelet, a puzzle, or a set of blocks —whatever your child is interested in. Show them that the world often feels like disassembled pieces—jumbled and mixed up. Things don't always make sense or seem fair, especially when people hurt us.

Work with your child to begin assembling the pieces. Explain that this is what God's work is like in our lives today. Remind them of what Jeremiah 29:11 says: that God has a good plan for our future. Explain that just as we are able to put pieces together to form a complete set, we can trust God is also putting things together to complete us. Share that we can begin to see the work He is doing now, and that we will see His perfect, completed work in Heaven.

End your time praying together over the thing that has been bothering your child. Ask God to help him or her see His rescue plan and to trust in Him. Thank God for His perfect plan and ask Him to draw near and comfort your child while he or she is going through a hard time. Thank God that He is always there to listen, guide, and comfort us when we pray to Him.

If we are

unfaithful,

He remains

faithful,

for He

cannot deny

who He is.

2 TIMOTHY 2:13 (NLT)

CHAPTER 2

Made for More than Rejection

 *Hagar*

I was bullied a lot in middle school. Whether for my stringy strawberry blond hair, my round rimmed glasses, or the splotches of freckles across my face, I was teased relentlessly for things I couldn't change. It also didn't help that I went to a small K-8 school, where the same kids who picked on me when the Pippi Longstocking movie came out in 1988 were the same kids picking on me nearly a decade later.

I managed to ignore most of what was said about me until one day in eighth grade. On this particular day when the lunch bell rang, I packed up my Jansport backpack, the one with all my favorite band names written in whiteout on the bottom. I headed immediately to my typical lunch spot and sat down. Just as I was mid-bite into my PB&J, a girl I'd been friends with since elementary school walked up and asked me to leave. When I asked why, she said the group had taken a vote and they'd decided they didn't want to be seen with a girl who "looked like" me anymore.

Ouch.

Rejection comes in a variety of forms throughout our lives. Maybe for you it was a best friend who stabbed you in the back, a parent who never made enough time for you, or a self-destructive boyfriend or husband. The wounds of rejection can leave us feeling like there's something wrong with us, like we just don't belong. We feel missed and misunderstood, and are often left wondering, "Does anyone really see me? Does anyone even care?"

We see similar experiences with rejection played out in the life of the first recorded single mother in the Bible, Hagar. Hagar's story appears in Genesis, alongside Abram/Abraham—the father of God's chosen people. Just before we meet Hagar, God promised Abram that he and his wife, Sarai, would bear a son. Just one problem with this promise—Abram and Sarai were *old*. Like, more likely to buy Depends than Pampers old.

After a decade passed and still no baby, Sarai got the hunch that maybe they need to "help" God. She cooked up a plan for Abram to marry and conceive a child with her much younger maidservant, Hagar.

Already, we can see that in Sarai's eyes Hagar was purely a means to an end. Sarai didn't care about Hagar—she only cared about what Hagar could do for her. And Hagar, being a young Egyptian slave, had no power to speak up for herself or avoid becoming a pawn in Sarai's game. Hagar was voiceless. Powerless. Invisible. Perhaps you have felt the same way.

What's worse; the plan actually worked. Hagar, who was probably closer in age to a senior in high school, was forced to marry a senior citizen. She quickly became pregnant. Despite not having a choice in the whole arrangement, Hagar actually became arrogant when she realized she'd been given what Sarai could never have—a child. This was the only power Hagar had, and she decided to use it to taunt Sarai and get back at her for what she'd done. As Hagar was about to find out, comparison can make us feel pretty powerful. But the truth is it just sucks us down into endless competition—the kind where nobody wins.

Sarai became vengefully jealous. She knew that as Hagar's mistress she still had the upper hand. Sarai decided she was going to make sure Hagar would never forget who held the real power in the situation.

As you can already see, this whole thing played out like a season of the Real Housewives of the Old Testament. Sarai harassed and abused Hagar to the point that the pregnant Hagar escaped into the desert. A pregnant woman thinking she'll be safer in the desert? It was that bad. Given the history between the two, I think this move on Hagar's part may have been one part "I'll take my chances on my own," and one part, "Let's see her have her baby now."

In a lonely, awful moment like this, I can imagine Hagar probably thought, "This is not fair. Does anyone care? Does my life even matter? Does anyone even know I'm alive?"

It's there that the angel of the Lord—a manifestation of the presence of God—appeared to her. He asked her, "Where have you come from and where are you going?"

Now God obviously already knew the answers to these questions. But sometimes, the point of a prayer is for us to experience what it's like to be heard by a God who loves to listen to us.

Hagar explained the scenario and the angel of the Lord comforted her. He gently assured her that what she was going through wasn't for nothing. God had a plan for her: He would raise up this abused, exploited, and outcast woman and make her into the mother of nations. And it wasn't because Hagar was so righteous or had it all together (she didn't), but because that is what God in all His goodness had planned for her.

But there was a drawback to all of this for Hagar. For God's plan to become a reality, Hagar had to go back to Abram and Sarai. Her circumstances would eventually change, but not yet. It wouldn't be easy, but as a reminder of the promise that Hagar still held, the angel of the Lord tells her to name her son Ishmael, which means "God hears."

In that moment, Hagar realized God had had His eyes on her all along. He hadn't forgotten her, but rather had been forging a plan for her the entire time. He had *chosen* her. And this would have been super surprising, because Hagar was not even born into the nation of God's chosen people.

God loves to bless the ones others would say don't deserve it.

Nothing Hagar had gone through had been beyond God's

view. Because of this, she declared to the angel of the Lord, "you are the God who sees me. Truly, here, I have seen Him who looks after me."

Sit in that truth for a moment. Hagar may have spoken these words, but God didn't just see *Hagar.* That's not who He was to *her alone*; that's who He is to all of us. To you. To me.

Hagar returned to Abram and Sarai (now called Abraham and Sarah), and after thirteen additional years, Sarah finally gave birth to Isaac, the child promised to her.

(I want to pause here and point out that Hagar was not the only one who received a promised blessing from God. Even though Sarah didn't have it all together, God had promised her a son too.)

Unfortunately, despite having the child she'd been waiting for, Sarah's jealousy returned. Ishmael was found teasing Isaac, and Sarah decided she'd had enough. Just as quickly as she had jumped into this whole thing with Hagar, she decided it was time to bail out.

Sarah's a little "You're hot then you're cold. You're yes, then you're no."

Scheming Sarah hatched another plan. This time, she demanded Abraham drop Hagar and Ishmael in the middle of the desert and leave them there for good. But where Sarah had a plan for evil, God had a plan for good. Abraham was crushed by the thought of losing his son, Ishmael, but God told Abraham to let it be so. What God had in store for Hagar was bigger than what her circumstances would allow. For God to give Hagar what He'd promised, she would need a whole lot more room.

Abraham obliged. He abandoned the pair and in an instant, Hagar became a single mom. What seemed to have been working out had been suddenly ripped away from her. Has this ever happened to you? In Hagar's mind, life was over. They would die, and the promises God had made to her would be lost.

Hagar found herself yet again in the desert, and she despaired when the water supply ran dry. I can imagine how those old thoughts must have crept back into her mind: "This is not fair. Does anyone care? Does anyone even see us?"

But in her doubting, God didn't shame her, and He doesn't shame us either. He didn't wag His finger at her and mock her for her lack of faith. Not at all. In fact, He did just the opposite. Again, He revealed Himself to her. He drew close to her. He comforted her. The God who had seen her all along was still there. And though things looked impossible, He hadn't changed a single thing. What she thought was punishment was actually positioning.

Suddenly, a well of water appeared. Hagar and the boy were refreshed, and Hagar's hope returned. Though they remained in the desert for some time, God continued to provide for Hagar and Ishmael. Ishmael grew into manhood in the desert and under God's watchful care, the promise that Hagar's descendants would multiply beyond what could ever be counted was eventually fulfilled.

We often think of people from the Bible as really holy, perfect people. We wonder why God would bother to appear to just anybody, let alone make great plans for them. But as we can see, Hagar wasn't perfect. She made mistakes. And even after God gave her the most incredible promise, she doubted. But God kept showing Himself to her. He blessed her with His closeness and kindness and He gave her a new path for her life that was bigger than the one she had envisioned for herself. He wanted Hagar to know she was seen, and that her life had great value to Him.

And the same is true for you too.

I can promise you this: God will give you bigger dreams for your life than you have for yourself. He is replacing what was lost—stolen—with something good, and a life better than you can imagine for yourself. I know it can be hard to see when you're in the middle of it all, but since the days of Hagar, God has been choosing cast-off, "rejected" women just like you and me for great things. And even when your faith to believe it runs out, He won't.

FOR FURTHER STUDY READ GENESIS 16, 21.

 *Memory* VERSE
"If we are unfaithful, He remains faithful, for He cannot deny who He is."
2 Timothy 2:13 (NLT)

The Greek word for "faithful" in this passage is *pistos* and it can be translated to mean "reliable" or "trustworthy." When someone is trustworthy, it means their good character is consistent over time and through lots of different circumstances.

And *pistos* is not passive—it's something that's backed up by actions. Trustworthiness is established when what someone *says* and what they *do* match up.

One of the things that is constant about our human existence is change. We change all the time, and so do the circumstances around us. This can be a good thing and a bad thing. While change can be very hard on us, it is a blessing in that change allows us the opportunity to grow.

But God does not change. He is always the same—always patient, always loving, always compassionate. In our world of change we can find that kind of consistency hard to believe, but that's also what makes it so refreshing to our exhausted and overwhelmed souls.

This verse tells us that even when we struggle to be consistent, God will not stop being exactly Who He is, nor stop showing that consistency through what He does. As the *Weymouth New Testament* puts it, "And even if our faith fails, He remains true. He cannot prove false to Himself."

Reflection QUESTIONS

1. How has the mistreatment or harm you've received from others in your life caused you to feel about your place in the world? Your place with God?

2. Have you wondered if God sees or cares about you and your kids?

3. Do you struggle with having waves of faith and waves of doubt? How do this week's selections help you understand where God is in that experience?

4. How does it feel to know that even when you doubt, God still desires to reveal more of Himself to you?

Practice: LAMENT

Remember that when the angel of the Lord first appeared to Hagar, he said, "Where have you come from and where are you going?" Even though God already knows the answers to these questions, God still desires for us to share with Him where we're coming from. When we spend time with Him and really get honest with Him, we get to experience what it is like to be seen, known, and loved on a one-to-one level by the God of the Universe. That's pretty incredible when you think about it.

Lament is one of the ways that we can tell God where we're coming from. Lament is basically prayerful complaining. In lament, we cry out to God about what is unjust, and we open our hearts to allow Him into the broken and messy parts.

Sometimes this can feel foreign or frightening. You may not be certain that all of your thoughts and emotions are presentable to God. But just as with Hagar, God will not turn you away, but rather meet you in your grief to reveal more of His love, compassion, and promises for the future.

God does not get tired of us. We can't wear Him out. And our complaints are actually the place we get to agree with Him about the things in this life that are wrong. It is then we can ask for His help and refreshing.

What is troubling your soul? Try these steps to pour out your lament to God:

» Tell God what is unjust, confusing, or frustrating about your situation.
» Share with God how you feel about it.
» Ask Him to make clear to you where He is in the midst of it all.
» Appeal to His kindness, justice, and mercy, that He would move on your behalf.

» Seek the wisdom to see things as He does, and for eyes to see what He will reveal.

» Request what you need to continue.

» Grieve what you have lost and receive His compassion as He grieves with you.

» Thank Him for promising to stay with you and carry you through.

WORSHIP PLAYLIST RECOMMENDATION
"He Has Time" by Common Hymnal

 *Family* FOCUS

START THE CONVERSATION

» Ask your child to think of a time when they had their feelings hurt or felt ignored. Ask if they ever feel like no one sees them or cares about them.

» Affirm your child's responses by expressing that you would probably feel the same way in their shoes. Commend them for the courage to share about hard things.

» Tell your child that you too have felt as they do. Describe a time when God revealed His closeness to you.

» Explain that God always sees us, and that He is always seeking after them. Remind them that God wants to show them His goodness, His kindness, and to bring them joy.

ACTIVITY

Grab a clear jar (jam, baby food, etc.), a pen, a piece of note paper, clear tape, and a bucket or large bowl of water. Ask your child to hold the empty jar, and to tell you if there is anything in it.

On the piece of paper, write down a word or phrase that describes something about God (for example, "God is faithful"). Fold the paper and tape it to the inside of the jar. Turn the jar upside down (no lid).

Next, submerge the jar in a bucket or large bowl of water. Make sure to go straight down and not at an angle or water will get in. You should be able to submerge the jar and the trapped air will stop water from entering the jar. When you pull the jar out, remove and read the note placed inside. You can then explain that while the jar looks empty, there is something in it that causes the water not to enter, and that something is air!

Just like we can't see air, but we know it's still there, we can also trust that God is present even though we can't see Him. Conclude your time praying with your child. Ask God to reveal Himself to your child. Ask Him to show them that He is always there to bring peace and comfort.

Now to Him who is able to do

exceedingly

abundantly

above all that we ask or think,

according to the power that

works in us, to Him be glory

in the church by Christ Jesus

to all generations,

forever and ever. Amen.

EPHESIANS 3:20-21 (NKJV)

CHAPTER 3

Made for More than the Bare Minimum

Naomi & Ruth

I received my first family heirloom when I was 18 years old. In the months after my great-grandmother's passing, my mother gifted me with a necklace she discovered as she was managing the details of Nana's estate. The pendant was an elegant silver starburst with a lone diamond in the center. It was a beautiful treasure, yet something simple enough to be worn every day.

I have a handful of memories of visiting my great-grandparents when I was young. To prepare for our visits, Nana would always save stale bread for my brother and me to feed the ducks in their neighborhood pond, and make a plate of gingersnaps for us to dig into when we got back. She also had that certain "grandma" smell (which I later found out was

Jean Nate perfume and cigarettes). Wearing her necklace always reminded me of those special times and I wore it a lot when she first passed.

Each time I wore Nana's necklace, I made sure to put it back in its velvet lined box for safekeeping. As time went on, I phased Nana's necklace out of rotation, but kept it safely tucked away. Several years (and apartment moves later), I was going through a photo album and noticed the necklace in a picture of my great-grandmother. I went to my jewelry box to find the necklace, but strangely it was not where I remembered putting it. I frantically checked another drawer. Not there. I scrambled to the garage to go through stacks of boxes (you know the ones you have shoved in a corner but never get around to unpacking). I was crushed when I realized that in all the moves and packing and unpacking, I'd lost the necklace. But what I'd lost was not just a precious heirloom; it was a piece of my grandmother's memory that I would never get back.

There are times in our lives just like this, when we are painfully aware of what we've lost, and what it's really cost us. For example, when you lose a partner, you may also lose in-laws, a home, savings, a job, neighbors, friends—not to mention life with your kids as you knew it or hoped it would be. In losing all these things, it becomes clear over time that you've actually lost so much more than another person. What you've really lost is a sense of safety, significance, security, and maybe even sanity.

And sometimes, it seems the losses just keep coming. When we look at all we've lost and the little it can seem we have left in comparison, it can feel like we are forever changed (and not in a good way). We may ask, "Is this all there is to life? What is left for me now?"

One woman from the Bible who walked through this experience was Naomi. We meet Naomi at the beginning of the book of Ruth. Naomi was an older widow who lived in a place that was not her homeland. Decades before, a much younger Naomi and her husband found themselves in the middle of a famine, and were so desperate to survive that they actually relocated and resettled in enemy territory, a place called Moab.

(Now I don't know if you're into football at all, but I am. And this would be like Packers' fans packing up and moving to Chicago. Major rivalry.)

Naomi and her husband did alright, at least for a while. They made a home, raised a couple of sons, and watched as their boys married Moabite women. They seemed to have escaped the worst. But then the losses hit Naomi hard. Her husband died; then her sons died–both of them. She became a vulnerable widow. As Naomi stared at the ashes of her life and what had been taken from her, she decided she'd be better off heading back to her homeland, alone.

And as you'd expect, she wasn't happy about it. She says in Ruth 1:21, "I went away full, and the Lord brought me back empty."

When Naomi looked around at her life, she was constantly triggered by reminders of all she had lost. She even told people to stop calling her Naomi, which means "pleasant," and instead told people to start calling her "Mara," which means bitter.

Honestly, sometimes I think Naomi gets a bit of a bad rap for this. She was so overwhelmed by the weight of her grief that just couldn't see the way forward. If you're reading this, I know you've been there. Maybe you're there right now. And if that's the case, I want you to know there is no shame in that. We do more harm than good when we ignore how we really feel and try to bypass our grief.

But there is something here that we have to pay attention to: Naomi was stuck. She'd made loss her permanent address; she'd made a home out of hopelessness. When Naomi looked around her, *all* she could see was what she lacked. She feared God had abandoned her and she worried that her future would look just like her past.

Can you relate? I know I can.

But then there's Ruth. Ruth was Naomi's daughter-in-law, the widow of one of Naomi's sons. When Naomi headed back to her homeland of Judah, Ruth decided to go with her. And this was actually pretty strange considering Ruth was originally from Moab.

Honestly, it would have probably been a whole lot easier for Ruth if she had just stayed in her native land. After all, she was born and raised in Moab. She could have easily started an essential oils business with all of her high school besties still living around her. She could have met a new guy through a friend of a friend and lived happily ever after. Why would she leave everything she knew behind?

Like Naomi, Ruth had lost a lot too. But when Ruth looked around at her life, she saw beyond what was right in front of her, and sensed the possibility that something more was still ahead for her. Though her husband had died, Ruth recognized she still had a life to live and decided it wasn't wrong for her to embrace that. So when Ruth looked at the future, she saw what she still had to gain.

Naomi and Ruth were two women in similar situations. But where one saw lack, the other saw limitless potential. Where one saw scarcity, the other saw possibility.

Ruth became Naomi's caretaker, and the pair of women went back to Naomi's hometown near Bethlehem. For two hungry and husbandless women they couldn't have showed up at a better time. They rolled into town at the height of the harvest season, and though they probably didn't arrive with much, Jewish law required field owners to leave a small percentage of their grain unpicked specifically so hungry widows could "glean" the fields and find food to eat. And guess who just "happened" to have a relative in town that owned a field? Naomi.

The relative who owned the field was a guy named Boaz. Boaz was actually related to Naomi's husband, and that mattered for a really specific reason—more on that in a minute. All they knew initially was that they might be safe in Boaz's fields, because he was known for being a good guy.

Oh, and did I mention he was single?

When we step back and look at the big picture here, it's clear that God led Ruth and Naomi to the right place at the right time. God had arranged everything in such a way that they had access to precisely what they needed in order to survive.

Ruth saw that things were aligning for her and Naomi, and she decided to head out and glean barley from the fields. This was pretty bold considering Ruth was an unmarried woman from a rival territory. She would have been pretty vulnerable, if not potentially unsafe. But Ruth saw opportunity, and she was there for it.

As Ruth gleaned, Ruth 2:3 says she "just happened" to end up in Boaz's field. Boaz noticed her. And what was not to notice? Ruth had an incredible work ethic and a heart for a woebegone former mother-in-law. Boaz was curious, but thought he was too old for Ruth to ever swipe right on him. But that didn't keep him from using what he had to help Ruth in her vulnerability.

Boaz extended a special kindness to Ruth and offered her a place at his feasting table. And to think Ruth came to the fields simply seeking *possibility*. What she found was overflowing abundance. Ruth 2:14 says she attended the meal and "ate until she was satisfied, and...had some left over." This was no ordinary all-you-can-eat buffet; Ruth ate until she was full *and* got to take home some leftovers.

Boaz didn't stop there; he sent Ruth home with ten days' worth of extra grain for herself and Naomi. Boaz was exceedingly generous to Ruth and Naomi, going far above and beyond what the law required of him in caring for widows. But that's just the man of character he was.

When Ruth returned home, she told Naomi all about Boaz's surprising generosity. As Ruth retold the story, a twinkle returned to Naomi's eye. Guess who saw possibility now!? Naomi suspected that Boaz might have had a thing for Ruth, and she encouraged Ruth to present herself to Boaz for the possibility of an engagement.

Now I know this seems a little sudden—after all, they just met. But remember what I said about Boaz being a relative of Naomi's husband? In Jewish culture, if a man died, it was the duty of an unmarried family member to marry his widow and keep his family legacy alive. This family member would have then been known as the "kinsman redeemer," and in Naomi and Ruth's case, Boaz was in line for the job.

Naomi was too old to be remarried to a kinsman redeemer, but Ruth wasn't. And if Boaz became Ruth's kinsman redeemer, it meant he had priority over the average Jewish man when it came to marrying her. Naomi knew this, and told Ruth just what to do.

Ruth presented herself to Boaz and expressed her interest in becoming his wife. Boaz couldn't believe that Ruth was interested in him—remember to this point he'd figured all the guys in her DM's were much younger than he was. As it turned out, Naomi was right—Boaz did have feelings for Ruth, but he never intended to act on them.

Boaz wasted no time setting things in motion, but there was one more issue that had to be sorted out. There was another guy in the family who actually had first dibs on the kinsman redeemer slot. But when Boaz talked to him about marrying Ruth, Boaz found out the guy was actually a diehard Green Bay Packers fan who had no interest in a woman from Chicagoland.

By now can we all say we do not believe in coincidences?

Boaz and Ruth married and had a son—but even that was not the end of the story. There's more. We actually see Ruth's name again later in the Bible, in The New Testament.

John chapter 1 starts off with a list of named ancestors in the family tree of Jesus. And guess whose name is right there in the middle of the list? Ruth.

Think of the magnitude of it all. This woman—a widow and an outsider—became the great-great-great-great-great-great (I'm not sure how many greats) grandmother of *Jesus*. God's redemption of her story is better than anything any human mind could possibly create. But this wasn't because Ruth went looking for a guy who would make everything okay again. She went in search of the life God still had for her, and Boaz was just the icing on the cake.

And Naomi wasn't left out of the mix. With a bouncing grandbaby on her knee, Naomi found joy in knowing her legacy would live on. In her old age, when it seemed least likely, God did not let her leave this earth without seeing redemption for her story as well.

Now, of course, none of this erased what Naomi and Ruth lost. Their pain was still a part of their story, as our grief is for us. But when all had been lost, Ruth dared to believe there was more for her, that *she* was made for more. Her expectancy prepared her for opportunity, which God used to provide for her and bless her. And Ruth's hope was contagious, bringing joy and prosperity not only to those around her but to all of us through Jesus.

Do you see the strong theme running through Ruth's story? *Her loss led her into surprising abundance.*

As far as we know, Ruth didn't have a miraculous personal encounter with God like Hagar did. But Ruth shows us just what can happen when we believe in the possibility that God still has more ahead for us and partner with Him to take back our lives.

FOR FURTHER STUDY READ THE OLD TESTAMENT BOOK OF RUTH.

> *Memory* VERSE
> Now to Him who is able to do exceedingly abundantly above all that we ask or think, according to the power that works in us, to Him be glory in the church by Christ Jesus to all generations, forever and ever. Amen.
> Ephesians 3:20-21 (NKJV)

The phrase "exceedingly abundantly" in this passage is actually one single Greek word: *hyperekperissou*. The root word, *perisseus,* on its own means "exceedingly." But in this word combo, we also see the prefix *hyper. Hyper* in this context means just what it does in our English usage—over, excessively, beyond.

This phrase tells us that God is able to do "beyond exceedingly" more than we could ask or imagine. And that's what we see in the story of Ruth.

Think back: if Boaz was generous in his kindness and favor, how much more is God? This passage also tells us that through God's "exceedingly abundant" work in us, His goodness and glory pass down to generations—down to our kids. God didn't just give Ruth and Boaz a son; but through that son (and the generations that followed) the blessing was multiplied and passed down to all of us in the person of Jesus. That's far more than Ruth and Boaz could have ever asked or imagined. That's *hyperekperissou*.

? Reflection QUESTIONS

1. Have you found yourself feeling like Naomi –as if all is lost and the future looks hopeless?

2. What has been lost or taken from you? How has this affected your view of God?

3. How do this week's selections impact any sense of hopelessness you have about your own future? Your kids' futures?

4. Consider this week's memory verse. What influences, past or present, make it hard for you to believe in God's "exceedingly abundant" power and goodness?

5. What would it look like for you to challenge those influences and dare to believe for more for your life?

 *Practice:* **SERVICE**

The baby boy born to Ruth and Boaz was named Obed. Obed means "servant of God."

Ruth moved to a new land with nothing to her name. She had nothing tangible to offer. But she did have an eye for opportunity, a tenacious heart, and able hands for physical labor. She used this unique combination of gifts and abilities to serve Naomi, and through her own two hands came an incredible work of God that we are all still benefitting from today.

Service connects us to God and others. When we serve, we open ourselves to experience God's abundant goodness as He works through us and the people around us. God takes even the smallest offering we can bring, and multiplies it into something more than we could ask or imagine.

Romans 12:6 says, "God has given us different gifts for doing certain things well." In the example of Ruth, we can see how powerful our service to others can be when it is connected to our God-given gifts and interests. We begin to truly experience fulfillment and joy in discovering precisely who God made us to be and where He's called us to use our gifts—even when that's in the middle of our mess. God wants to be expectant. And while we can't know exactly how God will reveal Himself, we can trust that He will.

If you haven't already, take a spiritual gifts test. Then, spend some time in prayer, talking with God about your gifts. Consider asking:

» When did I first notice these gifts?

» How have I used these gifts in the past to help others?

» How have I seen God move through these gifts in my life before?

» Have I used these gifts in ways that have glorified myself? How can I address that going forward?

» Who do I know that has similar gifts I can learn from?

» How can I grow in my confidence and ability to use these gifts to bless others?

» Who do I know right now that would be blessed by these gifts?

» What is the next thing I can do to grow in my relationship with God and others through my gifts?

WORSHIP PLAYLIST RECOMMENDATION
"Don't You Give Up On Me" by Brandon Lake

 ## *Family* FOCUS

START THE CONVERSATION

» Many times when we feel let down, disappointed, or hurt by people, it can impact the way we view God as our Father. Gently ask your child: "What do you think or feel when you hear the phrase 'God is a good Father?' Is it easy or hard to believe God is a good Father?"

» Let your child know you can understand why they would feel the way they do. If they express anger or disbelief that is not something you need to correct. Also, resist any desire to add to or expand upon your child's thoughts. Your focus is to create a safe environment where the child can express doubt and disbelief and allow room for their thoughts and feelings to develop over time. It is an important step in healing.

» Share that people on earth are fallen sinners and because of this, we can't love perfectly. But God is different. He has never sinned, made a bad choice, or broken a promise. We can trust that God is the perfect Father because He is holy and perfect.

» Explain that the same God who did miracles in the Bible is still active today. That He hasn't changed. It's normal to feel sad or frustrated when we are hurt or disappointed, but God sees us and can still do amazing things even in tough situations.

ACTIVITY

Grab a few scraps of paper, pens, and flower seeds. You'll also need a place for planting, like a plastic cup or flower pot with soil, or an outdoor space. Ask your child to write down on each scrap of paper something they have been hoping would happen, but hasn't. Write down your thoughts too. Allow your child to share or keep their answers private.

Explain that we all have dreams we hope will come true—some will and some won't. Though we may want something good, God wants what is best, and we can trust Him with our dreams because He sees what we don't see. Roll up the scraps of paper. Dig a hole five inches deep in the soil and bury the scraps of paper. Remind your child that God still sees what is written on the scraps of paper, and that even though we might forget about them, He won't.

Fill in the hole partway, covering the paper scraps but leaving room to plant the seeds. Plant the seeds and remind your child that just as we'll see beautiful things come out of the ground in time, we'll also see God bring beautiful things into our lives.

Pray that just as Ruth did, you'll both have the faith to wait on God's best, as He does far more than you could ask or imagine.

For the
anger of man
does not
produce the

*righteousness
of God.*

JAMES 1:20 (ESV)

CHAPTER 4

Made for More than Abuse and Mistreatment

 *Abigail*

When I set out to pursue a career in writing, I met with a literary agent who gave me a piece of advice I didn't believe when he first said it. He said, "If you write long enough, someone will try to take credit for something you've written."

The main reason I didn't believe this guy was that I honestly didn't think my work was worth copying in the first place. I thought, *Maybe he's just trying to be flattering.* But I also could not imagine someone having the guts to do such a thing. After all, we're talking *Christian* publishing, people.

But one afternoon as I was scrolling through one of my social media feeds, it happened. A quote I'd published in a blog post four years earlier was suddenly staring back at me through my iPhone. But what caught me off guard was the fact that the post wasn't a reshare of the one I'd originally created, but an entirely new image. The organization using the quote had put together their own graphic (emblazoned with their logo) without ever giving credit to the original source. Worse yet, the caption featured nothing but a link to the organization's website with a prompt to "Donate Now."

I knew I could file a complaint with the social media platforms, but I also knew how extremely pointless that would be. The post had been out for weeks, and the damage had already been done. I was certain this post had already been long forgotten by anyone who had actually viewed it, but to me this small act of plagiarism represented a violation of my honor and trust.

And I was powerless to do anything about it.

I know a stolen quote is small potatoes in the realm of betrayals (it's definitely small potatoes compared to my other experiences with betrayal). But when we are mistreated, we all experience some level of disgust, shame, and outrage. Perhaps you've extended your love, kindness, and care to another, only to find yourself taken advantage of and discarded. Not only is the experience painful, it's unnerving when we begin to realize this person has done this thing *on purpose*. In that moment, the entire world feels unsafe. And so often when this happens, we find ourselves powerless–unwilling or unable to speak up–for fear of the consequences that could come next.

Sometimes we look at what others have done to us and wonder where God is in the middle of it. We always hear "God is just," but when wickedness seems to get its way, we may not be sure how that really works out in our real lives. In instances where it seems we're left with no options and no way out, we might ask, "Is God going to do anything about this?"

I can imagine one woman from the Bible asking this same question. Her name was Abigail. We meet Abigail in the book of 1 Samuel, and discover she was the wife of a wealthy man named Nabal. Now God didn't want us to be confused about who this guy really was. Nabal's name in Hebrew means *fool*. Not sure what his mom was thinking at the time he was born since "fool" was probably not on the list of top baby names that year. And yet, this is precisely who he turned out to be.

Nabal is described in 1 Samuel 25:3 as being "harsh and badly behaved." He was mean. Greedy. Unreasonable. And everyone knew it. There are stories of several abusers in the Bible and Nabal is certainly one of them.

But Abigail was the exact opposite. The same verse that tells us how horrible Nabal was, also tells us how lovely Abigail was: she's described as being both "discerning and beautiful." Put simply, this was basically the biblical version of Beauty and the Beast. The Bible doesn't say how Abigail and Nabal ended up together, but it wouldn't be surprising if Abigail had had little say in the matter.

The not-yet King David was also a part of this story. While journeying with his men, David and his crew come across Nabal's sheep shearers. Now, it's important to note here that soldiers trekking through the desert were usually low on provisions and notorious for beating up shepherds and taking their lunch money. But not so with David and his men. They took in Nabal's shearers and even offered them protection from anyone who would have tried to take advantage of them.

As we saw with Ruth and Naomi, all of this happened at just the right time. It was sheep shearing season, and David assured the shearers that they and their flocks would make it home for the "end-of-the-shear" celebration. This was a big deal. As we saw in the story of Ruth, harvesting anything in this agricultural society would have meant a huge party was expected to follow. It was the agricultural equivalent of the Super Bowl, and everything was riding on these guys making it home.

(Yes, I know – another football reference. Shout out to all my sporty/ tomboy/ boy mom friends out there).

Hungry and tired (and probably dreaming of Buffalo wings), David sent some of his men back to Nabal's compound with the shearers. David instructed them to ask Nabal if he would be willing to return the favor of their kindness, and allow David and his men to join in on Nabal's shearing celebration.

This wasn't a big ask: David and his men had gone out of their way to make sure Nabal would still have had sheep to shear in the first place. And Nabal was stinking rich; surely he could have pulled together the extra place settings at his sheep shearing feast. But in typical "fool" fashion, Nabal refused. Actually, he completely embarrassed David and ridiculed him. When word finally got back to David, he was furious. In fact, he was so angry he gathered 400 of his fiercest fighters and they set out to destroy Nabal and his household.

Now I know Nabal was being hateful. But David's reaction was extreme. He was being a total hot head. But David wanted justice. And we aren't so different sometimes. How often does our own anger drive us to take matters into our own hands?

Abigail found out about the whole thing and couldn't believe what this husband of hers had started. But she knew the way to a man's heart is through his stomach, so she and her servants pulled together a lavish assortment of foods in the hope of convincing David to reconsider. If this were happening today, I imagine it would have looked as if she'd raided the inside of a Trader Joe's: she'd have the gourmet meats, the cheeses you cut with the fancy knives, and the crackers with the raisins inside.

Abigail set out with her gourmet buffet, and "just happens" to cross paths with David before he could make it all the way to Nabal's homestead. She apologized profusely and explained that her husband was exactly what his name implied—a fool—and asked that the blame be on her shoulders.

Honestly, this whole thing sounds like she'd had to take the fall for Nabal's stupidity before. She'd been conditioned not only to take Nabal's wrath, but to take responsibility for it. If you've been in an abusive situation, I know you understand where she was coming from. It's what she'd needed to do to survive.

Instantly, David saw the situation with fresh eyes. He realized that had he gone through with his plan, he would have slaughtered a lot of innocent people who were already enduring the oppression of a brutish master. He wasn't supposed to kill these people; he was supposed to have compassion for them.

David also realized that through Abigail showing up at just the right time, God Himself had intervened and kept him from committing some pretty horrible sins, all in the name of seeking his own form of "justice." It was apparent to both of them their meeting was not a coincidence. It was a divine appointment.

David told his men to fall back, and sent Abigail home in peace. When Abigail finally returned, she basically found Nabal kicking back in his recliner, Buffalo wings in one hand and beer in the other. He was drunk as a skunk and scarfing down a one-man feast, his face smeared with the same chips and dip that he refused to share with David.

What was Abigail thinking at this moment? I have to imagine she was humiliated, wondering if this scene was an indication of the rest of her life. Maybe she thought, "What did I do to deserve this? How is this ever going to be made right?" Perhaps she sighed deeply and headed to bed, figuring she'd just deal with it all the next morning.

Morning arrived and Nabal had sobered up. Abigail told him about her rendezvous with David. Why she volunteered this information—the text isn't clear. Perhaps Nabal had asked where she'd been; perhaps she thought he'd be proud of her for stopping the attack. Regardless of how this conversation got going, Nabal was instantly filled with rage over what his wife had done. But before he could lash out at her, he dropped like a rock. Nabal "mysteriously" suffered a stroke and died ten days later.

Except it's not a mystery. First Samuel 25:38 says that "*The Lord* struck Nabal, and he died" (emphasis mine). God brought about the justice that Abigail and David had been waiting for, in a way they never could have done themselves. And David gave God the glory, saying in verse 39, "Blessed be the Lord who has avenged the insult I received at the hand of Nabal," and "returned the evil of Nabal on his own head."

It's important to state here that this passage of Scripture does *not* imply that anyone in an abusive marriage should stay around and wait for God to take care of it. The Bible gives clear guidance that those being abused should seek safety, away from an abuser.* But given the culture, location, and era in history, Abigail did not have a way out.

What we *should* understand from this passage is that God does not tolerate the evil we suffer at the hands of others. The wicked are given the chance to repent, but when they don't God's justice prevails, in His way and in His timing.

And, of course, the story does not stop there. As we've seen before, with God there is always more. After Nabal's death, David sent for Abigail. He knew what a literal fool Nabal had been to take advantage of such an incredible woman. With Nabal out of the picture, David expressed his desire to marry Abigail. And this time, Abigail had a say. Faster than she could say "yes" to the dress, she hurried to be by David's side, and took her place as wife to the future King of Israel.

Though Abigail suffered greatly as Nabal's wife, that was not the end of her story. God brought rescue and justice in a way that everyone, both then and now, would understand that His desire is to set free anyone who has abused and mistreated.

FOR FURTHER STUDY READ 1 SAMUEL 25.

> *Memory* VERSE
> "For the anger of man does not produce the righteousness of God."
> James 1:20 (ESV)

When an injustice occurs, it is natural to feel angry. This kind of anger is not sinful–God Himself is angered when injustice occurs. Our emotions are given to us by God to indicate when we have a need. They are an invitation for us to turn to God, and find peace in His compassion for us, no matter the circumstances. When we are harmed, we have a need for protection and justice. And when we turn to God in our anger, we can trust that He will ensure our needs are met.

However, the problem is that when we sit in our anger, avoid dealing with it, or sweep it under the rug, it becomes a bitterness that leads us into retaliation. When we don't deal with our feelings or turn to God in our need, we, like David, have a tendency to take matters into our own hands and make justice happen on our own terms. Except that what results isn't actually justice.

The Greek word for "righteousness" in this verse is *dikaio-suné*, which also means "justice." This verse is telling us that human anger can never lead to the holy justice that God gives. In our anger, we are moved to injustice. But God in His anger is moved to true justice. For perfect and complete justice to be enacted, we must deny the urge to see things handled in our own ways. We must bring our anger to God and trust Him with the outcome.

As we see in the case of Abigail and Nabal, God did not tolerate injustice. Though justice may seem slow in coming, God's justice always comes at just the right time. He is perfectly patient in His anger, humbling the proud to repentance and delivering the wicked to defeat. We can be assured that whatever the timing or outcome, God's justice will be unmistakable and complete.

(?) Reflection QUESTIONS

1. What injustices in this life have made you feel angry? Do you have the tendency to sit in your anger or avoid it?

2. How have this week's story and memory verse given insight into God's justice and righteousness?

3. How has Abigail's story impacted the way you believe God views the things you have suffered?

4. Has your anger moved you towards further injustice? What would it be like to bring your anger to God and rely more on His compassion for you in your circumstances?

⊙ *Practice:* FORGIVENESS

Forgiveness can be difficult. From what we're often taught, it seems that when we forgive someone, we're saying what they did to us was okay. This is a common myth about forgiveness. Forgiveness does not turn a wrong thing into a right thing. Wrong is still wrong!

The Bible says that we don't fight against flesh and blood humans. When we are harmed by another person, we're actually being attacked by the powers of darkness that have infiltrated the other's life. Unforgiveness is a scheme of the devil to keep us locked in a battle against another human being, distracted and unaware while Satan pummels us spiritually.

When we fight evil with evil, we use the wrong weapons to engage in a war we can never win.

Forgiveness sets *you* free. Forgiveness is not something we feel but something we choose. In forgiveness, we call out the wrong that was done and identify exactly what it has cost us. In bringing these hurts and wrongs before God, we declare that we will not be the ones to exact revenge. We will entrust justice to Him in whatever way He chooses, and we find the strength to fight evil with goodness.

God may move the offending person to repentance, but if they resist, He may also allow their sins to pierce their own hearts. And though we may find some comfort in knowing God avenges us, it is wise to resist handing our enemies to Him with a "go get them, God" sort of a spirit. God's judgment is pretty hefty if you think about it, and the only reason we are able to avoid being in the same position as our offenders is God's gracious choice to rescue and forgive us. Forgiveness gives us the power to shake off the devil's attempts to drag us back into the battle, and remain in the shelter of God's loving protection while He does what only He can do.

The point is, in forgiveness we recognize that God is God and we are not. He sees things we don't and has plans we can't understand. When we forgive, we are entrusting ourselves to His infinite wisdom, so we can let go of what is not ours to handle. We make space in our hearts to heal, and in doing so, we will receive extraordinary peace, knowing that our God is for us and will not forget about us.

Forgiveness is something we can do with God in prayer. Prayers don't always have to be spoken—they can be written too. You may find it helpful to try out this practice using pen and paper.

Make sure you have a quiet space and lots of time to work with so you won't feel rushed. Start by asking God who it is that you need to forgive. Then make a list of those who have injured you. Choose one person from the list, and consider the following steps:

» IDENTIFY the source of the hurt. Name the person who hurt you and create a list of specific things they did or failed to do that injured you.

» ACKNOWLEDGE how this person's behaviors harmed you and how these things caused you to feel. Be detailed about what you lost and how their choices cost you.

» RECEIVE God's compassion. Sit in His presence, knowing that God is grieving with you over how you were wronged.

» STATE your choice to forgive. Tell God your desire to get far away from the devil's attempts to drag you into sin, and that in choosing forgiveness you are choosing the path of peace. Ask for eyes to see as God defends and restores you, bringing good where the devil has brought harm.

» ASK God for comfort and strength as you open your heart to healing. Ask Him for wisdom to know how to set boundaries with or separate from this person. Forgiveness is freely given, but trust is not. Reconciliation will not be possible until a person who has broken trust behaves in a consistently healthy and repentant way, which often takes years to establish.

» REPEAT. Forgiveness is a major part of healing, but it's not the only part. The wounds may still be fresh, and you may feel angry once again (especially if this person continues to hurt you). If you feel angry again, it doesn't mean you haven't forgiven, only that your head must remind your heart that this is now in God's hands. In time, the heart will eventually catch up with what the head already knows.

WORSHIP PLAYLIST RECOMMENDATION
"Ruins" Maverick City Music featuring Joe L. Barnes & Nate Moore

 *Family* FOCUS

START THE CONVERSATION

» Ask your child to think of a time when someone hurt their feelings, or a time when they felt really angry about the way a friend had been treated.

» Reflect back to your child what happened and how it made them feel. Let them know that God gives us feelings, like sadness or anger, to point out to us when something is wrong so we can find help.

» Share that while it's not a sin to get angry, not dealing with our anger will only cause it to grow into bitterness. Bitterness leads us into sins like retaliation that only make the problem worse. Share with your child examples from your life where you sought after your own justice and it backfired.

» Explain that forgiveness is the way God helps us deal with the feelings that come up when we are hurt. Explain that forgiving someone doesn't mean that what they did was okay, but that in forgiveness we give our hurt to God so anger and sin won't have power over us. If appropriate, share with your child how practicing forgiveness has helped you deal with your own hurt feelings.

ACTIVITY

For this activity, you will need a backpack and a stack of books. Ask your child to put on the empty backpack and notice the freedom they feel to move around as they'd like.

Explain that our heart is like the backpack, but that every time we are wronged, it feels like a book is added to our backpack.

Begin to place books into the backpack. If your child is comfortable sharing, as you place a book in the backpack have them name a hurt they've experienced in the past.

Continue filling the backpack until it is at a weight your child can manage, but with effort. Ask your child to walk around and notice the difference in their ability to move. Consider making a game of seeing who can carry the most books for the longest distance. When your child tires of carrying the bag, take it off.

Explain that just as you took the backpack off of them, God desires to free us from the hurts that weigh us down. When we forgive others, the books–the hurts–don't disappear. We hand them to God to take care of them. When we do, we are free to move around without carrying a heavy burden. We can trust that God will take care of us as He rights every wrong.

They triumphed

over him

*by the blood of
the Lamb*

and by the word

of their testimony.

REVELATION 12:11 (NIV)

CHAPTER 5

Made for More than What Has Happened

The Woman at the Well

I was not very successful when it came to dates for high school dances. While most of my friends always had a close guy friend or boyfriend to ask them out, I often found myself having to do the inviting if I wanted to go. I did always end up with a date, but not without an extremely high percentage of failed attempts (which most often looked like a guy saying "yes," then backing out two weeks later when he realized what he'd really wanted to say was "no").

Throughout high school, I wondered if something was wrong with me. *Why doesn't anyone want to invite me? What am I missing that the other girls have?* And truth be told, I know this played a huge part in me falling for an abusive relationship at seventeen, because I wanted so badly to believe that maybe for once someone had actually cho-sen me.

Sometimes we hear these miraculous stories in the Bible, or maybe the stories of people around us, and think, *Yeah, that's great. But that could never be me. My story is way too far gone and I don't have anything great to offer. This stuff doesn't just happen, at least not to people like me.*

We have all had these thoughts that at one time or another. And one woman from the Bible whom I think can probably relate is the "Samaritan woman"—also known as the "woman at the well."

This woman has received the "Mean Girls" treatment from the church for centuries. Even today when her story is told she's still often treated as gossip fodder: a forgettable, pro-miscuous woman rejected by her entire community. And while other stories in the Bible show that Jesus has deep compassion for anyone with sexual brokenness in their story, this woman's story offers us an entirely different experience of the Lord's kindness toward all of us.

Her story is found in John 4. One day around noontime, Jesus was tired and thirsty after teaching and traveling. While His disciples went off to grab some lunch, Jesus decided to stay behind and sat down at a well in the town they were passing through.

I should mention something about this town—it was in a region called Samaria. To Jews, Samaria was "the other side of the tracks." Samaritans were Jews that had long ago mixed bloodlines with their former captors, the Assyrians. Jews looked down on Samaritans for being inferior and impure.

When traveling in the area, Jews were known to go around Samaria rather than straight through it, even if that meant doubling the length of their trip.

But not our Jesus. Jesus comes for the ones everyone else avoids. As Jesus rested by the well, a woman of the town approached to draw water. Remember, it was the middle of the day—and let me tell you, after living in the Arizona desert for more than a decade, I can tell you the middle of the day is a pretty miserable time to be filling up your canteen. If that was the case, why was she coming to the well so late?

Some have suggested that maybe she came so late in the day because she was rejected by the women in town, who would have gotten together to draw water in the morning. However, there are clues from the text that would suggest this was not really the case (which I'll get to in a minute). It's very possible she had an entirely different reason for *choosing* to go alone in the middle of the day. (Hold that thought.)

Back to the story. Jesus turned to the woman and began speaking with her. He said to her, "Please, give me a drink." But she was a little more than guarded; immediately she retorted, "How is it that you, a Jew, ask for a drink from me, a woman of Samaria?"

Whoa, seems like a pretty blunt response. But from her shoes, this would be like Johnny Football Hero making his way across the cafeteria and striking up a conversation with the brainy girl with glasses and braces (I can say that because I was her in high school). She was suspicious, especially since Jews typically didn't think Samaritans like her were worth their time.

But of course, Jesus didn't feel that way about her. But she didn't know that–yet. He went on basically to say, "You don't know me, but I'm not like the rest. If you knew more about me, you'd know that I have living water, a water that completely refreshes and satisfies. It's the water of life, and if you knew it was for you, I think you'd probably be asking me for a drink."

She was confused. What was this guy even talking about? She couldn't grasp the concept of living water and I doubt we would have been able to either. All she saw was the world and the way things were–in black and white. This Jewish guy wasn't really supposed to be talking to her, and she couldn't tell whether He was the real deal or a door-to-door salesman trying to take advantage of her by selling her a vacuum she didn't need.

Though she was suspicious, she was curious–He wasn't like the rest. The woman basically responded, "What do you mean? You don't have a rope or a bucket or anything that could be used to draw water out of this well that's right in front of us. How in the world do you think you're going to get this living water?! And who are you that you have access to this special life water anyway? Are you some kind of holy guy or something?"

I can imagine Jesus probably smiled at her when she started asking about who He really was; in her heart, she knew He was different and she wanted to understand. She had her suspicions, but those suspicions were leading her to ask all the right questions about Him. And that's how God sees us in our moments of doubt; He's not afraid of our questions because our questions lead us right to where He can be found.

Jesus told her that the water she's thinking about—physical water—does need a ladle and bucket, but that living water doesn't. He explained that living water actually bubbles up from inside a person to refresh them, and when they experience it they won't be thirsty again.

At this point, they were talking about two different things. She was still thinking about things in the physical world—things as they are. But Jesus is talking about the spiritual world—things as they should be, as He was making them to be.

At this point in the story, we might just think, "Jesus, why all the vague answers? Just tell her *you* are the living water!" But to be honest, she probably would not have believed Him if He had. How many times have you had to teach your child a lesson by guiding them toward figuring it out for themselves? Things stick a little better that way sometimes.

What she said next was a bombshell: she said, "Sir, give me this water, so that I will not be thirsty or *have* to come here to draw water."

Have to come here to draw water? This phrase is more loaded than we realize. *Having* to come to this well was an *inconvenience* to her, and not just because she had to lug her gallon jugs back and forth every day. After all, it's not like people at this time had somewhere else more convenient to get water; going back and forth to this well was just a part of everyday life back then.

So if this was not about water jugs, then what was the inconvenience really about? What was she trying to avoid? It's far more likely that the reason she didn't want to *have* to go to the well anymore was that she was lugging around something far heavier than water jugs. She was lugging around a broken heart.

Jesus knew that in stating that she didn't want to *have* to go the well anymore, the woman was revealing there was something more below the surface. He knew she was cracking the door open to reveal the brokenness of her story, even if just slightly. Maybe she didn't even realize what she'd said, or maybe she hoped maybe He wouldn't pick up on it.

She was almost there, almost to the point of freedom, but Jesus knew she'd have to take one more step before she would open her heart fully to receive what He had for her. He plays along, giving her the last prompt she needed to step into a life-changing encounter with His compassion, though He knew it would be a painful one for her. He basically says, "Okay then. Why don't you get your husband, and then come back here?"

Uh, oh. She's caught.

In making a comment that was a little too specific, Jesus had just pinpointed the cause of this woman's broken heart, the reason why she'd been so guarded in the first place—the shame of her singleness. I believe at this moment, she knew He knew, and she may have sensed that perhaps she'd said far too much.

For many of us, we'd be triggered by this scenario, and we might do everything we could to slam that door shut again. Maybe we'd try explaining it away. Maybe we'd peace out and forget the whole living water thing. And in this moment, she had a choice to make; she could either hide what He clearly already knew, or find out what would happen if she opened her heart and let someone in.

She took the risk. She replied, "I have no husband." What a moment of courage and vulnerability as this once guarded woman let her walls down.

Jesus gently responded, "You are right in saying 'I have no husband.' For you have had five husbands, and the one you have now is not your husband."

For too long, Jesus has been depicted as calling her out for being a girl who would just "love them and leave them." However, if this woman truly had been promiscuous, the law would have required her to be stoned, like in the story of Jesus and the woman caught in adultery. This Samaritan would have been stoned to death long before she could have ever had five husbands.[4]

(What's more, John wrote both stories; the story of the woman caught in adultery appears just four chapters after the story of the woman at the well. If the Samaritan woman had been an adulteress like the other, John probably would have mentioned it.)

So what was really going on here? What if this woman hadn't left five husbands, but she'd been left *by* five husbands?![5] Based on the customs of the time, it's reasonable to assume she'd been divorced five times; something only husbands and not wives could do at the time. Childlessness was a valid reason for divorce at the time, so it's possible she had been repeatedly discarded by men who thought, "It will be different with me," but then left her by the roadside when she couldn't conceive.

It's also possible that in some of these marriages, she could have been widowed.[6] Whether she was infertile, widowed, or both, she would have been seen by the people around her as cursed by God for all of these tragic outcomes of her marriages. They believed if bad things happened to you, it was because you'd done something (or your ancestors had done something) to deserve it. She wouldn't necessarily have been rejected and outcast by her community, but she definitely would have been the woman people whispered about when she walked by.

When Jesus pointed out she'd had five husbands, He wasn't trying to shame her; He was acknowledging where she already felt ashamed.[7] He was saying, "Daughter, I know what's happened. I understand where you're coming from. I know the whole story already. And I'm here for you."

Through this interaction with her, Jesus was demonstrating for all of us what happens when we get really honest with Him; He wants us to know we can expect His gentleness and compassion. If we will open up the door to our hearts–to our hurts– He will pick up what's weighing us down and exchange it with freedom. Sadly, that never comes through in the old interpretations of this passage. Jesus is so much better than we know.

Jesus also revealed in this statement that the man in the Samaritan Woman's life at the time of their meeting wasn't actually her husband either. Again, what was Jesus trying to point out here by saying this? To grasp what was happening, we have to put ourselves in her shoes. Remember, she's been left husbandless five times. *Five.* By the fifth time, how worthless and forgotten do you think she felt?

With five dissolved marriages, she may not have had

many great options for a husband at this point; the "good guys" probably would have been nervous about getting involved with a girl who had a history like that. As a result, perhaps her expectations were so low that she was willing to settle for a lazy man who wouldn't even show her the dignity of making her a proper wife. Maybe this was the only kind of relationship she'd ever known, and didn't think there could be anything better. Maybe she'd just decided she wasn't really marriage material anyway. Whatever the case, with each failed relationship her self-esteem and hopes would have been in steady decline, to the point she had likely accepted her circumstances as "just the way things are." Things with her current guy weren't ideal, but at least she wasn't alone.

I can definitely relate to that.

Five absent husbands, a lazy boyfriend, and no hope in sight. This woman had a pile of reasons why she didn't want to *have* to go the well anymore. With all that had happened to her, she may have started believing the whispers of the townspeople–that something was wrong with her–and perhaps she began pulling away to avoid the humiliation of it all. Truth be told, when our lives go from good to garbage we just might prefer that table by ourselves in the cafeteria too.

But God won't let us self-isolate. He won't let us be swallowed up by shame. He comes for us and tears away the darkness that covers us. But we have to decide–are we going to hang onto it, or let it go? Are we going to dare to reject the lies and see ourselves the way He sees us? That we are worthy of unconditional love, right where we are?

Though Jesus had exposed her woundings, the woman dared to draw closer. In seeing herself as Jesus saw her, she also began to see Jesus for who He really was. How could He have known the details of her past and yet extend such grace? She was captivated by the combination of His gentleness and greatness. She figured He really must be a holy guy after all!

She didn't know if she'd ever see this guy again, and since he obviously had some heavenly connections and was willing to spend the time talking to her, she began asking Jesus big questions about life and faith. When she got around to asking what Jesus knew about the coming Messiah, Jesus responded:

"I who speak to you am He."

It finally clicked. The reason He knew so much, the reason He wasn't fazed by her ethnicity or her story—the woman realized she'd been speaking to the Christ, the Holy One of God.

But who was she that Jesus would reveal His true identity to *her*? She couldn't believe it. She ran back to town and gathered up the people saying, "Come see a man who told me all I ever did! Can this be the Christ?"

Not only did they willingly follow her, but John 4:39 says, "Many Samaritans from that town believed in Him because of the woman's testimony." Had she been a rejected outcast as once believed, the people probably wouldn't have responded like this—they probably would have thought she was out of her mind. But because they knew her story and pitied her for her terrible luck, they were intrigued—how could someone so stricken by God be given such a revelation?

Jesus used this average, everyday moment to transform the brokenness of this woman's story into a powerful testimony. He used what had held her down to lift her up, restoring a reputation that had been otherwise dragged through the mud.[8] Jesus did not choose a man of high status or nobility to carry His message to her people; He chose a woman no one else would have chosen. And in doing so, He showed all of us that in His Kingdom, the ones who seem to have been forgotten about are actually the first in line.

Jesus absolutely came to rescue all of us for all eternity. But He also came to rescue us in the here and now. He wants to make clear that no matter what you've been through, no matter what has happened, the circumstances of your life do not have the power to change who you are to Him—*chosen*.

FOR FURTHER STUDY READ JOHN 4.

Memory VERSE

They triumphed over him by the blood of the Lamb and by the word of their testimony.
Revelation 12:11 (NIV)

In a court of law, a testimony is an eyewitness account—the story of what we've seen and experienced in our own lives.

In this verse, the Greek word for testimony is *marturia*, and it means "evidence" or "what one testifies to." This verse declares that we have already triumphed over the enemy—for all eternity–because of Jesus' atoning blood shed for us. It also states that there is overcoming power in our testimonies, the everyday evidence of God's intervention in our lives in the here and now. Your story is a weapon; a counterattack against the enemy of your soul. The devil wants to see you silenced. He wants to see you so discouraged that you can't see all that God is doing right now.

We already know how the story finishes–we win. But how can we know what that feels like in the here and now? Sometimes we look at the hard parts of our lives and assume that this is how it all ends, and we just have to tough it out until Heaven. But God is working through the tough stuff to give you a story redeemed by His power and goodness–and this verse promises that.

God wants us to look for Him in everything around us, because He is revealing His redemption in real time. When we do, our faith is strengthened as we realize that this really is the truth – He really is making all things new.

Sometimes they are little "God winks," small experiences that you know could only be Him. Other times, they are big moments when the odds are stacked against you . . . but God. Whether big or small, these moments come together as evidence of God's presence and power in your life

Maybe it's despite the circumstances. Maybe it's because of them. But through it all, the goodness of God gives us a new story to tell.

？ Reflection QUESTIONS

1. What have you previously been taught about the woman at the well? Has your perception of Jesus and/or the Samaritan Woman changed?

2. How has pain or shame from the past caused you to think less of yourself, lower your standards, or isolate from others?

3. How does seeing Jesus' compassion for the woman's story impact the way you believe He sees yours?

4. How does it feel to think of your story as a powerful weapon against the enemy? Where have you had limiting beliefs about what God is still doing in your story?

Practice: REPENTANCE

Depending on how you were raised or what you've been taught, the word "repentance" can stir up some difficult feelings. I grew up in a legalistic tradition, and just the mention of the word opens a floodgate of memories. Often those memories are of times I felt ashamed and condemned.

But that's not the heart behind the biblical usage of the word at all. The Greek word for repentance in the New Testament is *metanoia*, which purely means "to change your mind." When we repent, what we are really doing is changing our minds about going our own way, and instead choosing to agree with God and His ways.

The woman at the well allowed Jesus to change her mind—not only in what she thought about herself, but also in this relationship she'd settled for.

And when Jesus changed her mind, He also changed her story.

Romans 2:4 says that God's kindness moves us to repentance. This isn't about condemnation, it's about kindness that brings clarity—seeing things as God sees them and choosing His way.

Repentance isn't something we do for God to make Him approve of us, but something we do with Him as He leads us back to His side.

God knows what truly is best for us. After all, He created us and knows just how we are designed! Being made for more means getting honest about what we have been settling for that's outside of God's design, and seeking His help to turn away from the sins that are holding us down. It's there we begin to discover what more He has in store.

Consider these steps in a prayer seeking repentance:

» ASK the Holy Spirit to reveal areas of your life where you are not in agreement with God and His ways. Ask what is keeping you from knowing a closer relationship with Him, and what you need to turn away from.

» ACKNOWLEDGE the specific thoughts and beliefs that have led to you choosing to go your own way instead of God's. Consider asking when you first believed these things. Grieve how you came to these thoughts and beliefs, and accept responsibility for your part in how you have allowed them to take root in your life.

» ADDRESS the harm that has come from doing things in ways that are in conflict with God's ways. Be specific about your choices and actions, and how they have impacted your relationship with God, the way you treat yourself, and the well-being of other people.

- » THANK God for the forgiveness He has already extended to you through Jesus and take a moment to receive His unconditional love for you.
- » INVITE the Holy Spirit to guide you in turning towards new thoughts and actions that are in agreement with His ways. Consider asking what one next step you can take.
- » PRAISE God for His closeness and kindness.

Any time you feel distant from God, consider a prayer of repentance to find out if there's something that is blocking you from connection with Him. And don't worry if you don't feel forgiven. Just as offering forgiveness takes practice for our hearts and minds to be in sync, receiving forgiveness can too.

WORSHIP PLAYLIST RECOMMENDATION
"Until Grace" by Tauren Wells and Rascal Flatts

 *Family* FOCUS

START THE CONVERSATION

- » Sin is choosing to go our own way, instead of God's way. Ask your child to think of a time when they decided to do something they knew was wrong. How did they feel about it before? After? What were the consequences?

» Explain that consequences are God's way of getting us back on the right path. They aren't meant to hurt us, but to lead us in a better direction. God's ways may not always make sense and may not be what we want; but He sees things we don't see and wants what is best for our hearts.

» Share that "repentance" is the word the Bible uses to describe getting back on track. Talk about a time when you went your own way and wandered from God's path. Describe the consequences and what you learned about choosing to repent and go God's way instead.

» Reassure your child that you are a person they can talk to whenever they make a mistake, and that you are always there to help them get back on the right track. Consider praying with your child, asking God to guide you both as you walk His path together.

ACTIVITY

Take your child outside on a sunny day and have them sit comfortably. Ask them to notice the sun. Can they feel it? What do they notice about the way it shines on things around them? Explain to them that the sun is like God's love for us. It is always there, shining down on us and all around us. Share that when we pay close attention to His presence, we can feel His love in our hearts just as we feel the sun on our skin.

Now, ask your child to put up a barrier to block the sun. They can move to a shady spot, or use a jacket or umbrella to shield the sun. Once the barrier is up, pause for a few seconds and then ask them how quickly they felt the sun's warmth lessen? Explain that our sin is like a barrier. When we sin, we often feel far from God, and don't sense His love the way we usually do.

Now, ask your child to remove the barrier and let the sun shine on them again. How quickly did they feel the sun's presence again? Explain that God's love and forgiveness is like the sun—it doesn't go away even when we put up a barrier. Discuss how removing the sin barriers from our lives and turning back towards God allows us to feel His love for us once again as we get back on the right track.

So let's not get tired
of doing what is good.
At just the right time

we will reap
a harvest of
blessing
if we don't give up.

GALATIANS 6:9 (NLT)

CHAPTER 6

Made for More than Your Mistakes

 *Eunice*

I still cringe when I think of the total "dance mom" I used to be. My oldest daughter started competitive dance around eight years old, and both her instructor and I quickly realized she was very gifted. I wasted no time going all-in with her—intensive private lessons, extra at-home practice sessions, anything we could do to ensure she'd rise through the ranks quickly.

We crisscrossed the country going to competitions, and she won trophy after trophy (some nearly as tall as she was). But as she became more competitive on stage, I became more competitive off stage. I started giving way more critique than encouragement, all in the name of "helping" her improve (you know how we do this sometimes). When her friends were swimming in the hotel pool, I insisted she stay behind and get a good night's sleep. And when she wanted to look at the sparkly socks and headbands at the vendor tables, I directed her back to the practice floor to get ready for her routine. Of course it wasn't *all* bad, but it wasn't all good either.

When my daughter first started dancing, she dreamed of one day competing on the World Championship stage. But by the time she hit fifth grade, all she could talk about was quitting. I pushed back; I figured it was a phase. After all, she'd been trying to cope with our cross-country move and unexpected divorce, and I didn't want her to give up on something she was so good at only to regret it later. But one day, I drove her to practice and she refused to get out of the car. After twenty minutes of prodding, I knew there was nothing more I could do. She was done. And while to this day neither of us regrets her quitting, I still regret it was the only way I finally recognized that I'd lost sight of what really mattered—my daughter's heart.

Often, we may find ourselves grieving over things that have been done to us, things that were outside of our control. But at other times, we might find ourselves full of grief and regret over the things we have done—mistakes we have made that we can't take back. Worse yet, not only are we left to deal with the consequences of our choices, but our kids may be too.

I know many times I have thought, *It makes sense that I have to deal with the fallout of my choices, but why should my kids have to suffer?* There are so many things I wish had I had done differently, even if only to spare them the heartache.

There's another woman in the Bible, another single mom, who I'm sure must have thought the very same thing. Her name was Eunice. Not much is written about Eunice, but here's what we do know: Eunice was a Jewish woman who lived around the time of Jesus, though her home was quite a bit farther to the northwest in what is now modern-day Turkey. Though Eunice was Jewish by birth, for some reason she ended up marrying a Greek man. How this happened is a bit of a mystery since Jews marrying non-Jews was a no-no according to Jewish law.

Whether it was an error of Eunice, her parents, or both, this mistake had some major consequences. Being a non-Jew (the Bible uses the word *gentile*) meant her husband did not share her faith in God; he was an unbeliever. Through this marriage, Eunice became "unequally yoked" to a man who did not share her same beliefs, values, practices, traditions, and overall viewpoint on life—something the Bible still cautions all of us to avoid.

(There's a good reason why the Bible encourages us to form our closest relationships with other believers. Being unequally yoked is somewhat like being in a three-legged race with someone who is not going in the same direction. Have you ever been in a relationship like that? I sure have.)

The issue of being unequally yoked hit especially hard when Eunice and her husband decided to have kids. Eunice gave birth to a son named Timothy (if that sounds familiar, he's the Timothy in 1 and 2 Timothy). We don't know much about Eunice's faith life, but though she was born a Jew, we do know that somewhere along the line she became a follower of Jesus. But Eunice's husband didn't; he was a pagan who did not even worship the One True God, let alone follow Jesus.[9]

And it appears that the way Timothy's father saw it, no boy of his was going to grow up following the rituals of a God he didn't believe in. Greeks hated circumcision, and as such Timothy wasn't circumcised in childhood as Jewish boys were supposed to be. This likely would have left Timothy feeling like an outsider in the Jewish community—he may have even been treated like one.[10]

And what's more, because Timothy's father was Greek, that meant Timothy was only half-Jewish. To the Jewish community, Timothy would have been considered ritually and ethnically impure. Timothy may have had a hard time finding a place where he fit in, a place where he truly belonged.

How confused do you think Timothy was, growing up in the middle of two worlds like this? Perhaps you are seeing this very same thing in your own children's lives. And I can't help but think of Eunice's mama heart, and how disappointed she must have been. Here was a woman who loved Jesus, married to a man who could not—would not—support her efforts to raise her son in the ways of the Lord.

Like so many other women in our study, Eunice had a choice to make. She could have spent her life regretting the circumstances she found herself in, or she could work with what she had left and trust that in God's hands, it would be enough to make a difference. And we know what she chose because we wouldn't be talking about her if she'd chosen to just give up and let the mistakes of the past have the final say.

Eunice decided it was up to her to teach Timothy the Scriptures and point her son toward Jesus. And I'm sure she had to have one Heaven of a prayer life, praying this boy would not grow up and choose the influence of his father.

(When I get to Heaven I'm going to have Eunice over for coffee. I think we'd have a lot to talk about.)

We don't know what became of Timothy's father, but at some point it appears he exited the scene. Whether he died or abandoned the family is unclear, but in his absence, Timothy flourished in his faith.

So how do we get to the point where Timothy ended up with not one but *two* books of the Bible named after him? Well, the Apostle Paul was kind of a jet setter, and during his travels he found out about Timothy. Though Timothy was a young guy, he already had a stellar reputation with other followers of Jesus in the area.

I think Paul probably saw some of himself in Timothy. Timothy was a young man growing in influence, but that influence could easily be corrupted without proper guidance. Paul met up with Timothy and decided to take him under his wing, making him somewhat of an apprentice. Here was Timothy, a boy born into the least impressive of circumstances, now being chosen to carry the flame of faith along with the Apostle Paul himself.

Can you imagine Eunice's joy as she saw all this unfold? Despite the lack of a godly biological father in Timothy's life, Eunice watched her boy become a man of God right before her eyes. God had taken what little Eunice had to pour into her son and multiplied it dramatically.

(Kinda like another story you may have heard of before, involving some loaves and fish. Wink.)

And here's the thing. This didn't happen because Eunice was the perfect Christian or came from the perfect family. She didn't have the perfect home life. She probably didn't lead perfect devotions. But you know what she did have? *Faith in a God who specializes in turning mistakes into miracles.*

While Eunice could not go back and change the past, the book of 2 Timothy says that Eunice had a "sincere faith" that "dwelled" within her. Instead of worrying about what she didn't have or the mistakes that were made, Eunice instead made room for God to shape her choices going forward. She allowed God to work first in *her* heart and *her* home, and dared to believe it would be enough to give Timothy a better future.

And, of course, there's more. Paul didn't just see Timothy as his protégé; he considered him a spiritual son. He made sure Timothy was finally circumcised– not because it had anything to do with his salvation (it didn't), but because it meant Timothy would finally be fully accepted by the Jews with whom he was called to share the Good News. Timothy would finally have a place where he belonged, and sense the pride of *two* fathers, a spiritual one (Paul) and Heavenly One (God, the Father).

Two books. Two fathers. As we've seen in so many of these stories, only our God can do multiplication in what looks like subtraction.

Eunice probably had a pile of regrets and disappointments about the mistakes of the past. We all have things we wish we had done differently; things we're not really sure God can fix.

But Timothy became the man God intended him to be—not in spite of Eunice's choices, but because of them. And though the road could not have been easy, Eunice saw the redemption of her past as she clung to the belief that God would not waste a single element of her story—not even the mistakes.

FOR FURTHER STUDY READ ACTS 16; 2 TIMOTHY 1

Memory VERSE

So let's not get tired of doing what is good. At just the right time we will reap a harvest of blessing if we don't give up.

Galatians 6:9 (NLT)

When it comes to raising our kids, we may know what the right things to do are, but we may wonder if they are actually doing any good. The Greek word for "good" in this verse is *kalos*, and it means beautiful, lovely, and praiseworthy. This is a good that inspires others and is in it for the long haul.

This verse declares a promise—when we focus on making our hearts and homes places where good is planted, those seeds will sprout up and become a harvest of blessing. But in the meantime, it may not feel so much like blessing.

As a child, did you ever plant a seed in a cup of dirt? Perhaps at first you were excited to see what would happen, only to have the thrill wear off when it seemed like nothing was happening. When you plant something, you can't watch the work that's being done underground. You can't dig up the seeds to see what's going on. And even once sprouts do pop up it still takes a lot of cultivating before that tiny seedling becomes a mature plant capable of bearing fruit.

When we don't see progress, it is easy to feel discouraged. But when we continue to cultivate good, God promises it won't be wasted. Maybe we see it on this side of eternity; maybe we don't. But when it comes to matters of faith, we do what we can do knowing God is at work doing things we can't see. He multiplies our offering, making so much more out of the little we bring. It's the way of the Kingdom, and it's just the way He is.

Every time you are tempted to worry about the timing of the harvest or the outcomes of your efforts, share with God what's on your heart. Talk with Him about what He would have you do together to build a life that's truly *kalos*—lovely.

Reflection QUESTIONS

1. What grief are you carrying about your past choices? What fears do you have about the way they are impacting your children?

2. How have the difficult things you've gone through helped you become the person you are? How have they

strengthened your gifts? What good things have come as a result?

3. Do you ever worry that your past is an indication of how the future will go? How do this week's selections help you see the possibilities that rest in entrusting God with what you have?

4. What is one thing you can do this week to focus on what you can do with what you have right now?

Practice: GRATITUDE

When circumstances are difficult, we often realize just how out of control our lives are. We may do what we can, but still experience a whole lot of anxiety as we worry about whether or not God is going to come through, fill in the gaps, or turn things around. Philippians 4:6 says, "Don't worry about anything; instead, pray about everything" (NLT). But have you done this and still felt like your prayers were bouncing off the ceiling and falling to the floor?

We often stop short when quoting this scripture, but that's not the end of the verse. Philippians 4:6 adds another ingredient to the mix that we often miss. It goes on to say, "Tell God what you need, and thank him for all he has done."

Now, I think I'm pretty good at telling God what I think I need, but when things look bleak it can be really hard to be thankful for what He's already done.

What does giving thanks have to do with dealing with our anxieties? When we give thanks to God—for the times in the past when He came through, for what we do have right now, and for what He promises for the future—we stomp out the lies that tell us God doesn't care or that He's forgotten. Thanking God reminds us of who He really is and the fact that He does not change. He is who He has always been, and we find reassurance in knowing that's who He'll always be.

It's through presenting our prayers and practicing gratitude together that we find peace for our anxious souls. Philippians 4:7 continues, saying, "Then you will experience God's peace, which exceeds anything we can understand. His peace will guard your hearts and minds as you live in Christ Jesus."

Sometimes we struggle with gratitude because we feel so overwhelmed with where we are right now that we forget to take time to remember. Think back on the story of Exodus, when God parted the Red Sea to rescue His people. Despite having experienced this miracle first hand, the Israelites had a hard time remembering all God had already done for them once they were in the desert—when things were really hard and uncertain. And because they refused to remember, they doubted who He was and what He was promising them. People like to bag on the Israelites, but ya'll, we are the same.

So at the end of their desert season, the Israelites ended up on the banks of another body of water. After 40 years of wandering, all that stood between them and the Promised Land was the River Jordan. But the River Jordan was deep, and they didn't have nearly enough floaties to get the Ark of the Covenant across.

So God does again what He'd done before—He causes the water to peel back and the Israelites walk across on dry land. Only this time, God instructs His people to do something unique to mark this miraculous river crossing to help them remember.

Before God brought the waters back together, He told the people to grab twelve stones from the dry riverbed, one for every tribe of Israel. These stones were then used to build a monument on the other side of the river, which became a physical reminder of what God had once again done for them.

This practice was repeated in the book of 1 Samuel when the Israelites defeated their fiercest enemy, the Philistines. Only this time, Samuel actually names the memorial stone. He calls it "Ebenezer," which means "stone of help."

God is our rock and our help.

You might find it helpful to create your own physical

reminder of the times when God has been your help and showed you His goodness. Consider gathering 12 stones and writing a word on each that symbolizes a moment for which you are grateful. If you don't have 12 stones, you might draw 12 images of stones on a sheet of paper and write a word on each, or simply create a list of twelve things you are grateful for using calligraphy pens or special paper.

Put the item you've created in a place where you'll see it. You could place the stones on a porch or patio, or post the drawing/ list inside your closet or in your bathroom.

Spend some time bringing your anxieties to God and giving Him thanks for the times He's revealed Himself to you through what He's done. Take a moment to receive and rest in His peace as He listens intently to you.

WORSHIP PLAYLIST RECOMMENDATION
"Just as Good" by Chris Renzema featuring Ellie Holcomb

 *Family* **FOCUS**

START THE CONVERSATION

» When we don't know how the future is going to turn out, sometimes we feel nervous. Ask your child to think of something they might be nervous about, whether past, present, or future. Affirm your child, letting them know that it is normal to feel nervous when we don't know what is going to happen.

» Discuss that even when we can't know the future, we can look back at all the things God has done before and know that He's still bringing goodness into our lives every day. Tell your child about a time when you were uncertain about how something was going to turn out, and what good you saw God do in it.

» Spend a moment with your child, remembering times when things seemed to just "work out." Connect the dots for your child, explaining that things don't work out on their own—that God is behind every good thing that comes into our lives.

ACTIVITY

Ask your child to gather stones, or you can provide stones they can use for this activity. Explain that each stone represents something in their lives for which they are thankful. Ask them to think of anything they enjoy, whether it's a physical item, a person or animal, or a special memory. Point out that everything good in their lives is a gift God has specifically given them to enjoy, and that God delights in giving these gifts.

If you have a child who loves arts and crafts, invite them to paint or decorate the stones with whatever you have on hand. If that is not your child's preference, suggest they write the name of the thing they are grateful for on each stone, or allow them to choose to leave them blank.

Next, have your child place stones around the house, near the things for which they indicated they are grateful. For example, if your child is thankful for basketball, they can put a stone next to their ball or hoop. If they are thankful for their family, they can put a stone near a family photo. Tell them that when they feel discouraged or it seems as if nothing good is happening in their lives, they can look at these stones and remember how God has provided before, and that He's not done providing yet.

Conclusion

*"Anxiety is a result of envisioning
the future without Me."*

From "Jesus Calling" by Sarah Young

The mid-afternoon sunlight of a crisp, autumn day poured through my office window as I sat in front of my laptop computer, my desk covered in unanticipated medical bills. Though I'd endured a battery of very expensive medical tests, the only thing I had to show for it was the sizable dent in my bank account.

With no answers, only one thing was certain: more tests would be ordered and my wallet would be getting even lighter. With Christmas looming just weeks away, I grew more anxious with each bill I received. Before pressing "Pay Now" on yet another invoice, I took a deep breath and uttered a feeble prayer: "Lord, I know you've got me, but I don't know how this is all going to work out."

At just that moment, a single cardinal peeked his head

out between the twigs of a now leafless bush beneath my office window. Cardinals are kind of a "thing" between God and me; He often sends one at just the right time to remind me of His closeness. At the sight of this little visitor I grinned, because although my circumstances had not changed this at least seemed to be a heavenly "read receipt" of my exasperated prayer.

As I rested in the moment, suddenly I noticed a second cardinal swooping in to join the first. Then a third popped into view beneath them. I couldn't believe what I was seeing; God had sent one cardinal many times before, and occasionally two. But three?!

The trio hopped out of sight, and I carefully crept across the room to peer out a second window to see if perhaps they'd perched upon a different bush. There, the original three had now joined three other cardinals! My eyes darted to try to take in the scene as several additional cardinals joined the flock. In my attempt to count them all I lost track, but I think I counted nine, maybe ten, cardinals. And then as quickly as they'd all appeared, they were gone.

The moment was fleeting, but powerful. I praised God through happy tears, fully aware that He had orchestrated this moment just for me. In the middle of my stress, I sensed God saying, "I know you're worried. But I'm right here."

Goodness doesn't always look like we think it will. That's part of the reason trusting God can be so scary—we know His ways aren't our ways. And because we can't predict what He's going to do we're afraid to hope, for fear of being hurt or disappointed all over again.

We like being able to define good for ourselves. We like things on our terms. It seems safer that way. But somewhere along the line, things inevitably break down. Our formulas stop working. And when that happens, we have a choice: we can keep doing things as we've always done them or let God show us what He says is good.

The hardest part of this whole ordeal is the fact that letting God define "good" often means letting go of what we think is good. Not easy. There was definitely a time in my life when I would not have thought seeing ten cardinals at once was all that "good," especially not when I still had bills to pay. It took losing my version of good (and life as I knew it) for a moment like that to still my heart and bring me to worshipful tears.

Sometimes we hold back from God because we aren't sure we're going to like His version of good. But what if in letting go we discover we actually have so much more to gain? Because here's the real of it: God is not asking us to let go of our version of good only to leave us wanting. He's not like a parent holding back dessert in favor of force feeding us spiritual broccoli. He's inviting us into a kind of good we can truly count on, that is never in short supply and can't ever be taken. He's showing us a good we can *expect* to be met by in each and every moment of every day, regardless of what we're facing. It's the kind of good that gives us a glimpse of Heaven here on earth as we walk confidently into the unknown, fully relying on the love of a God who is for us, with us, and in us.

This is the *more* that you and I were made for. Until you've experienced it, I can't adequately explain it. But I can tell you that despite the fact that I'm still living a story that did not go as planned (with its unexpected bills and lonely Friday nights), this life of *more* is absolutely available to all of us.

So with that, I will end on this–it's your turn to find out for yourself. I have a sneaking suspicion you already know what your next step is and may have a sense of what is holding you back. You might still be wrestling with *why* things happened in the past. You might be fearful about *what* is going to happen in the future. At times, I am too. But when *why* and *what* threaten to paralyze our steps, there's another question we can ask: Lord, will you show me *where* you are in this? Will you show me *where* you are in my story?

Then watch and listen. I'll bet the answer will feel something like, "I'm right here."

He may show up in a flock of cardinals, a well-timed Instagram post, a check in the mail, or a kind word from a friend. The treasures of His goodness are already all around you. And when you ask God to reveal *where* He is, you'll be surprised by how much *more* you begin to see.

> *Even though I walk through the valley of the*
> *shadow of death,*
> *I will fear no evil,*
> *for you are with me;*
> *your rod and your staff,*
> *they comfort me.*
>
> *You prepare a table before me*
> *in the presence of my enemies;*

you anoint my head with oil;
my cup overflows.
Surely goodness and mercy shall follow me
all the days of my life,
and I shall dwell in the house of the LORD
forever.

Psalm 23:4-6

WORSHIP PLAYLIST RECOMMENDATION
"Good to Me" Audrey Assad

NOTES

1. Dr. Dan Allender "*Setting the Stage*," https://theallendercenter.org/about/allender-theory/accessed January, 2023.

2. Dan Allender, "*To Be Told: God Invites You to Coauthor Your Future.*" Waterbrook Press, New York, NY 2005. .

3. Dr. Dan Allender "*Setting the Stage*," https://theallendercenter.org/about/allender-theory/accessed January, 2023.

4. Kristy McLelland: *Jesus and Women*, Lifeway Bible Studies, 2022.

5. Dr. Lynn Cohick: *Women in the World of Earliest Christians*, Baker Book House: Grand Rapids, MI, 2009.

6. Ibid. McLelland, *Jesus and Women*.

7. Endicott, Charles, *Commentary for English Readers*. Gospel Publishing.

8. Ibid. McLelland. *Jesus and Women*.

9. Ibid. McLelland. *Jesus and Women*.

10. Ibid. Endicott, *Commentary for English Readers*.

More from PlusONE Parents

Safe Haven: A Devotional for the Abused & Abandoned

Three words every abuse survivor must hear: **God hates abuse.**

The Christian Single Moms Podcast

On all podcast streaming platforms and YouTube

Red Flags in Dating: What They Mean (& How to Make Sure You Don't Miss Them)

Digital Class

FIND THESE RESOURCES AND MORE AT
WWW.PLUSONEPARENTS.ORG

Made in the USA
Las Vegas, NV
26 December 2024

15371639R00066